World Leaders

The Dalai Lama

rourke biographies

World Leaders

THE DALAI LAMA

by
LOUIS G. PEREZ

Rourke Publications, Inc.
Vero Beach, Florida 32964

Library of Congress Cataloging-in-Publication Data
Perez, Louis G., 1946-
   The Dalai Lama / written by Louis G. Perez.
      p.   cm.   — (Rourke biographies. World leaders)
   Includes bibliographical references and index.
   Summary: A biography of the Tibetan leader, discussing
his religious and political life.
   ISBN 0-86625-480-3 (alk. paper)
   1. Bstan-'dzin-rgya-mtsho, Dalai lama XIV, 1935-   —
Juvenile literature. 2. Dalai lamas—Biography—Juvenile
literature.   [1. Bstan-'dzin-rgya-mtsho, Dalai lama XIV,
1935- 2. Dalai lamas.]   I. Title. II. Series.
BQ7935.B777P47   1993
294.3'923'092—dc20
[B]   92-38325
                                                          CIP
                                                           AC

Contents

Color Illustrations

World Leaders

The Dalai Lama

Chapter 1

A Man of Peace

On a high plateau near the Himalayan Mountains, bordered by India, China, Nepal, and Burma, is the land of Tibet. The Himalayas are the highest mountains in the world, and Tibet has been called the "roof of the world." Geographically, Tibet is a remote and isolated land. Through most of its long history, its people have had little contact with the outside world. Many of the Tibetan people are simple peasant farmers, but until China invaded Tibet in 1950 there were other groups as well. There was a class of nobles who inherited their positions; there were thousands of Buddhist monks; there also were, and still are, nomadic people who travel with their herds of animals and live in tents made of yak hair.

The major religion of Tibet is Buddhism. The country's religious life and political life are strongly intermixed. Since the 1400's, the leader of Tibetan Buddhists—and the most important leader in the country—has been known as the Dalai Lama. Dalai Lama is a religious title that comes from the words for "ocean" (*Dalai*) and "teacher" (*Lama*). The title has sometimes been loosely translated as "Ocean of Wisdom."

There have been fourteen Dalai Lamas since the tradition began more than five hundred years ago. Tibetans believe that each Dalai Lama is the reincarnation of the previous one. In other words, they believe that the soul of each Dalai Lama is reborn into the body of the next.

The man who was to become the fourteenth Dalai Lama was born in 1935. While still a baby, he was tested by Buddhist leaders. When they decided that he truly was the Dalai Lama, he was given the name Tenzin Gyatso. He was

The Dalai Lama speaking at Indiana University in 1987. (AP/Wide World Photos)

four years old. He spent the next twelve years of his life in almost total seclusion while being raised and educated by Buddhist monks.

In 1950, Communist China invaded Tibet. Because of the threat that this posed to Tibet's people, the Buddhist leaders decided that it was time to name Tenzin Gyatso as the leader of Tibet. He was only sixteen years old. In 1959, the Tibetans tried to revolt against the Chinese. The revolt failed, and Tenzin Gyatso had to flee the country. He settled in an Indian village called Dharamsala in the Himalayan foothills. There he established a government-in-exile. For the next thirty years, he worked tirelessly to find a peaceful way to free his people from Communist Chinese domination.

The Nobel Peace Prize

On December 10, 1989, the fifty-four-year-old Dalai Lama of Tibet walked across the stage in Oslo, Norway, to receive the Nobel Peace Prize. He was wearing the traditional simple red robes of a Buddhist monk. Was this smiling, unassuming man, with his shaved head and eyeglasses, really the "god-king" worshiped by millions?

For thirty years he had been a god-king without a country. For thirty years he had been separated from his homeland by the snowcapped Himalayan Mountains and by the powerful army of the People's Republic of China. Since March of 1959, the Dalai Lama had been worshiped and adored by the nearly 100,000 fellow Tibetans who shared his exile as well as by the seven million Tibetans held prisoner in their own homeland by the invading military forces of Communist China.

For those thirty years the winner of the 1989 Nobel Peace Prize had been the focus of an intense international debate. One group saw the Dalai Lama not only as a peaceful holy man but also as the hopes and dreams of millions of poor Tibetans who were being brutally destroyed by the Chinese

Communists. Another group—mostly Communist governments allied with China—portrayed him as an evil man who abused the very people he was supposed to be leading.

World Reaction: A Holy Man

To many people, the Dalai Lama was very much like the peaceful Indian holy man Mahatma Gandhi. Gandhi, in the first half of the twentieth century, had led the Indian people in resisting English domination through the nonviolent method of "passive resistance." Despite the fact that the Chinese army had tortured and killed more than a million Tibetans since 1950, the Dalai Lama continued to preach forgiveness, tolerance, and peace. Year after year he called upon the nations and peoples of the world to settle their differences peacefully. Year after year he gathered people of different religious beliefs together to pray and to work for peace. He represented the dream of world peace to millions of Buddhists, Christians, Jews, Moslems, and Hindus.

For thirty years, this Tibetan monk clothed in simple Buddhist robes appeared in countries all over the world to speak to almost anyone who would listen. His message was always the same: that freedom for captive Tibet was the first step toward the creation of peace in the world. In many ways this Buddhist monk seemed to represent the living conscience of the world community.

When Egil Aarvik, chair of the Norwegian Nobel Peace Prize Committee, presented the Dalai Lama with the coveted prize, he suggested that this simple monk was the model for world leadership and that "his gospel of nonviolence is the truly realistic one, with most promise for the future."

World Reaction: A Chinese Internal Matter

On the other side of the debate were the various Communist governments who referred to the Dalai Lama as "the wolf in monk's clothing." They argued that he represented a brutal and backward system that robbed, raped, and ravaged the enslaved Tibetan people.

They maintained that while his people had starved in their dirty huts, the Dalai Lama ate expensive delicacies served by

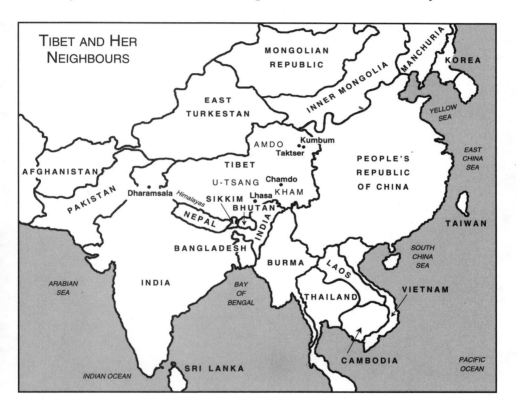

slave girls in his golden palace. These helpless Tibetan peasants, they said, had been freed from his harsh rule by their Chinese "brothers" and were now farming their own land, educating their children, and enjoying the fruits of their labors high in their remote mountain homes.

The Communist world argued that Tibet is a part of China

and that every attempt by the Dalai Lama to split his people away from "the motherland" was treason. The Nobel Prize was nothing more than an attempt by greedy Western nations to divide the people of China.

The week that the Dalai Lama was awarded the Nobel Peace Prize, the English-language Chinese newspaper *Beijing Review* published an editorial titled "The Deplorable Actions of the Nobel Committee." It suggested that the awarding of the prize to a man who wished to bring back a "theocratic dictatorship of monastic autocrats and nobles" was perhaps the "most disgraceful act in the history of the Nobel peace prize committee." The Czechoslovakian newspaper *Rude Pravo* called the award an "interference in China's internal affairs."

Who Is the Dalai Lama?

Somewhere in the middle of this argument, between the worship and hatred of this world figure, lies the truth about Tenzin Gyatso, the Dalai Lama. Who is he? Why does half the world love and respect him and the other half hate and fear him?

Chapter 2

A Baby Found in the Wilderness

In order to understand who the Dalai Lama is, one must first understand something about the Buddhist religion of Tibet. Buddhism teaches that the human soul continues to live on even after the body dies. The soul is reborn, or "reincarnated," into another body. Depending on what kind of life the person has lived, the soul is either reborn into a lower form of life (such as an insect, a mammal, or a bird), into a human baby, or as a god. When the souls of very holy persons are reborn as human babies, they must be discovered and replaced into their former positions of authority.

The Dalai Lama and Reincarnation

Tibetan Buddhists believe that these babies should be treated differently than common children because of the good that they have done and the wisdom they acquired in their previous life, or incarnation. Until the Chinese occupation of Tibet destroyed Tibet's traditional religious practices, these holy babies were taken to live in one of the hundreds of monasteries that dotted the Tibetan countryside. There, they were brought up to be Buddhist monks. Often they would become *lamas*—people who have completed a traditional three-year religious retreat. Lamas are believed to be wiser and holier than common people. Some lamas took part not only in the religious government of the temples and of the thousands of monks who lived there, but also in the political administration of the country.

The thirteenth Dalai Lama, Thupten Gyatso, who was born in 1876 and died in 1933. (AP/Wide World Photos)

The Dalai Lama is the highest-ranking lama in Tibet. All fourteen Dalai Lamas are believed to be the same "manifestation" of the Buddhist saint (or *bodhisattva*) named Avalokiteshvara, called Chenrezig in Tibet. Avalokiteshvara is the embodiment of compassion, a very important element in Buddhism, and is revered by Buddhists throughout the world.

When the thirteenth Dalai Lama died in 1933, a national search was begun to discover the next incarnation of his holy soul. It was believed that magical signs and omens would give the lamas sent to search for him hints about where to find the baby into whom the soul of the departed Dalai Lama had been reborn.

The Temple with the Turquoise Roof

One such sign involved the embalmed body of the thirteenth Dalai Lama. According to Tibetan custom, the body had been placed facing south. However, observers reported that the body continued to turn its head toward the east. Another sign was provided by holy men called oracles, who in trances could predict the future. They said that the fourteenth Dalai Lama was to be found somewhere in northeastern Tibet.

After a night of praying, the temporary leader (called a regent) of Tibet went to Lhamoi Latso, a sacred lake high in the mountains. Fifty years before, the searchers for the thirteenth Dalai Lama had received instructions there on where to find him. This time the leader had a vision in which he saw the Tibetan letters *ka*, *ma*, and *a* rise to the surface of the lake. He also saw a temple with a turquoise-colored tile roof and a path leading to a small peasant hut with a curious rain gutter made of juniper wood.

After nearly a year of searching, one of the many search parties happened to stumble into the province of Amdo (represented by the letter *a* in the vision), far to the northeast, where the turquoise-colored Kumbum (the letter *ka*) temple was. Close to the famous Buddhist hermitage of Karma Shar-ston (the *ma* stood for the second syllable of Karma) in the tiny village of Taktser, in a hut with a curious juniper-wood rain gutter, lived a family with a very special baby.

This baby was already famous in the region. From the time he could talk, he told anyone who would listen that his home was really in Lhasa. Also, he insisted that he, instead of his father, should sit at the head of the family table.

The search party learned that strange and unexplainable things had happened just before and after the baby was born in July, 1935. Both the father and mother had seen strange visions, and the father had become deathly ill. However, at the very minute that the baby was born, the father became well and had never been sick again. This region of Tibet had just gone through four years of very bad harvests, but, once the baby was born, the area had enjoyed unusually good harvests. Neighbors also told of the strangely beautiful rainbow that had seemed to touch the house of the baby at the time of his birth.

Testing the Baby

Yet before the now two-year-old child could be declared the reincarnation of the Dalai Lama, the infant had to be carefully tested. In order to avoid attracting attention, the search party disguised themselves as traveling merchants before starting to test the baby. It was believed that the reborn soul, while still a baby, remembers things about its previous life. Therefore, the members of the search party showed the baby many objects, some of which had belonged to the thirteenth Dalai Lama. When offered several choices, the baby always correctly identified "his" possessions—that is, those that belonged to the thirteenth Dalai Lama, his previous incarnation.

Several times the baby selected the correct walking stick, ceremonial drum, and old, worn Buddhist prayer beads. He chose these instead of shinier, more colorful, and newer

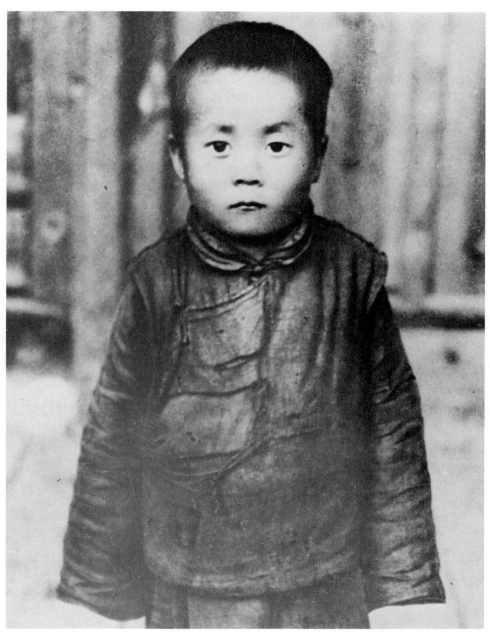

The Dalai Lama at age four, before being installed as Tibet's spiritual leader on February 22, 1940. (AP/Wide World Photos)

objects that might have attracted the eye of a normal infant. In one test, the baby seemed to hesitate when offered two almost identical walking canes. The reason for this was discovered later. The first cane he picked up had been the property of the thirteenth Dalai Lama, but he had given it to another lama. The second cane, which the baby finally took and refused to give back, was the cane that the thirteenth Dalai Lama had used until he died.

Unlike the rest of his family, the baby saw through the search party's disguises and said that the men were "lamas from Sera," indicating correctly the Sera Monastery from which they came. Finally, when the search party prepared to leave, the two-year-old baby ran around the tiny cottage gathering his few toys and clothes. He insisted that he was going "home" to Lhasa.

The Line of Succession of Dalai Lamas

No.	Name	Birth	Death
1	Ge-dun grubpa	1391	1475
2	Ge-dun Gyamtso	1475	1543
3	Sod-nams	1543	1589
4	Yon-tan	1589	1617
5	Nag-dban Gyamtso	1617	1682
6	Tsaus Gyamtso	1683	1706
7	Kal-bzan	1708	1758
8	Jam-dpal	1758	1805
9	Lun-rtogs	1805	1816
10	Tsul-Krims	1819	1837
11	Kas-grub	1837	1855
12	Prin-las	1856	1874
13	Thupten Gyatso	1876	1933
14	Tenzin Gyatso	1935	

When the testing was complete, the search party was convinced. The child's family also accepted that their baby was the reincarnation of the Dalai Lama. They agreed to move to the Potala Palace in Lhasa, the capital of Tibet.

Payment of Ransom

Before they could do so, however, Ma Pu-feng, the Chinese Moslem warlord who controlled the area, heard about the discovery of the Dalai Lama. He demanded huge bribes for the "protection" of the child. The government of China, which claimed that Tibet was part of its territory, also tried to intervene. Nearly two years of negotiations and compromises were needed before everyone agreed that the child could leave for Lhasa. Finally, a plan was devised. To be sure that the warlord and the Chinese government would not continue to ask for more money, a group of merchants promised to pay the Chinese their huge bribe only after the baby was safely in Lhasa. The merchants would then be repaid by the Tibetan government.

The baby, his parents, two sisters, and two of his four brothers made the trip to Lhasa along with the search party and the traveling merchants. Along the road, peasants heard that the Dalai Lama was passing. Many people traveled hundreds of miles to see him. The procession had to slow to a crawl for the last several miles of the journey as thousands lined the path, crowding to catch a glimpse of their infant god-king.

The people would not let the party pass until the child blessed them by laying his chubby little hands on their foreheads or by touching the traditional white scarves used for such blessings. All the people were impressed by the dignified way that this child, who at other times could be very mischievous, would quietly perform these blessings. It seemed to be another sign that this really was the reincarnation of the Dalai Lama.

Finally, the party arrived in the holy city of Lhasa, where the baby was renamed Jetsun Jamphel Ngawang Lobsang Yeshi Tenzin Gyatso. (He is now known by the last two names.) He was installed on February 22, 1940, as the fourteenth Dalai Lama and the manifestation of Avalokiteshvara, or Chenrezig. Because he was still a child, a regent, or protector, was appointed to rule in his place. For the next ten years, while the rest of the world was involved in World War II and its aftermath, the young Dalai Lama lived a peaceful if somewhat lonely life high in the remote mountains of Tibet.

Chapter 3

The Dalai Lama in Training

Once the five-year-old boy was safely in Lhasa and away from interference by the Chinese, the high lamas began his education and training. He was separated from his parents, but for three years his brother Lobsang Samten, who was three years older, was allowed to live with him in the palace.

A Mischievous and Lonely Boy

The young Dalai Lama was by nature a bright, curious, and, in many ways, mischievous boy. He was not very interested in learning the two different alphabets used by the Tibetan people—or in studying in general. He much preferred to romp and play like other children his age. Except for his brother, however, he had no playmates. The stern lamas and monks who were his teachers often had to chase him down before they could get him to sit and study for a few brief moments. His frequent allies in play were the young men who had been hired to keep the palace clean. He would wrestle with them or chase them about the palace in any spare moment.

His homes in Lhasa were the winter palace, the Potala Palace, made of stone, and the much smaller summer palace, the Norbulinga Palace. Actually, most of his boyhood was spent in only a few cold rooms in the Potala Palace, where he spent many lonely nights making friends with the mice that scurried about looking for crumbs.

The Potala is a huge 250-year-old stone fortress, seven stories tall, built atop the highest point in the Lhasa valley. Although the Potala is a beautiful and majestic place, the Dalai Lama later would say that it was "not a nice place to live." In addition to the living quarters, it contained a large temple and hundreds of other rooms. They were used for the government, for other monks who lived there, and as storerooms for the accumulated wealth of the thirteen previous Dalai Lamas. With more than a thousand rooms, it was by far the largest building in the world when it was built.

The Potala Palace, where the young Dalai Lama lived and received his religious training. (AP/Wide World Photos)

The young child much preferred the sunnier and cozier Norbulinga, mostly because it was closer to his parents' home and therefore he could visit them more often. It was also much more fun and interesting to a young child than the cold and formal Potala. The Norbulinga had a large garden and an enclosed park where tame deer, goats, monkeys, camels, parrots, peacocks, cranes, and geese wandered about. There was also a small zoo where some wild animals, including a leopard and a tiger, were kept.

Since his parents lived nearby, he would occasionally sneak away from the palace to eat tidbits such as dried meat, which was forbidden at the palace. Buddhism teaches that all life is sacred (because all living things are tied together through reincarnation), so most Buddhists do not eat meat. The young Dalai Lama developed a protective feeling toward animals later in his life and would often "ransom" animals on their way to be slaughtered for food. He would buy them and have them released in the wild.

Clocks, Toy Soldiers, and Old Cars

Although at first the young Dalai Lama was not a particularly good student, he was fascinated with mechanical things. The British government had sent him a gift of a Meccano set, which was a mechanical building set (something like steel Lego toys). He spent long hours building fanciful robots, cranes, airplanes, and automobiles. He also had a great love for clocks, which he immediately began to take apart to see how they worked. By the time he was ten, he could successfully reassemble them. He soon became an expert clocksmith, an interest that would continue into adulthood. At first, the few Tibetans who owned clocks hid them whenever he came into a room, but later they would bring broken clocks for him to fix.

Another of his favorite toys was a set of lead toy soldiers, which he neatly arranged in rows only to knock down in imaginary battles. Whenever he could convince or bribe his young servants to "play soldier," he would order them about, march them off to battle, then shoot them down with make-

believe guns. In a storeroom at the Potala, he discovered two
ancient hand-cranked movie projectors. He was determined to
get them to work. After questioning almost everyone in the
palace, he discovered an old man who knew how to run them.
The two spent countless hours taking the projectors apart, then
oiling, cleaning, and reassembling them. Finally, they
managed to view the few dusty films that they discovered
among the gifts given to the thirteenth Dalai Lama. One of the
films showed the coronation of the king of England.

Among the other long-forgotten "treasures" that he
discovered in the dusty storerooms of the Potala were two
pairs of European-style shoes. He promptly stuffed the toes of
one pair with rags so they would fit his small feet, and
clomped around noisily. He found many old guns and sabers,
as well as an air rifle, with which he secretly became an expert
shot.

By far the most interesting items for the young boy were the
three old automobiles—a 1931 Dodge and two 1927
Austins—that had been the property of his predecessor.
Despite the fact that Tibet had no roads designed for cars, the
Dalai Lama again scoured the palace for anyone who knew
about these run-down antiques. He found the man who had at
one time served as the driver. After many weeks of hard work,
the young Dalai Lama and his driver together managed to get
one of the Austins to run, and he would not rest until the day
when the two paraded majestically through the courtyard.

One day when the driver was away on other business, the
young boy climbed into the car and managed to drive it around
the garden. Unfortunately, he drove it into a tree, smashing one
of the headlights. Secretly he cut a replacement piece of glass,
which he smeared with syrup to make it look like the original
tinted glass. No doubt the boy could be a "holy terror" and a
danger to everyone in the palace as long as he was in the mood
for experimentation and adventure.

Beating the Goat to Scare the Sheep

Because the lamas believed that the boy was the reincarnation of the Dalai Lama and the manifestation of the bodhisattva Avalokiteshvara, the problem of disciplining him must have been a difficult one indeed. After all, how could they spank a saint? It might be wrong to harm such a saintly soul even if it happened to be reincarnated as a naughty little boy.

The lamas who were his teachers tried various methods to correct his behavior. Primarily they scolded and tried to shame him by threatening to tell his parents when he was mischievous. They also kept two whips mounted on the wall, one silk and the other leather. The first was to be used to spank him if he did not behave. The other was for spanking his brother. Unfortunately for poor Lobsang Samten, he would often be spanked when the two boys were in trouble, and the Dalai Lama would only be warned that he would be next if he did not behave. The lamas called this practice "beating the goat to scare the sheep." They hoped that the Dalai Lama would mend his ways when he saw his brother being punished.

The Debate Dance and the Education of a Lama

The more formal education of the young boy, once he finally mastered the alphabets and the rudiments of reading, was in the Buddhist holy writings. The common method of instruction was to memorize whole passages from the holy sutras (something like the books of the Bible), then to practice writing by copying them. Finally, the meanings of the sutras would be debated and discussed.

Tibetan Buddhists are very democratic in their approach to their religion. Young monks are encouraged to challenge and debate the views of their elders in formalized, almost dancelike discussions. Monks take turns sitting while others stand over them and hurl challenges at them, much like a pitcher throws the ball to a batter in baseball. The challenger stands with his left arm extended toward the sitting monk. He then brings his right hand smartly down into the palm of his left hand in a karate-chop motion, while stamping his left foot for emphasis. As he does so, he blurts out his argument.

Long lines of paired monks might spend hours hurling arguments and opinions back and forth in a kind of stylized and ritualized dance. The young Dalai Lama enjoyed this, at least partly because of the physical activity involved.

Why Can't I Be Like Other Boys?

As the young boy matured and began to pay more serious attention and care to his studies, he showed a flair for the debate dance. He became an expert. It was clear to his teachers that he was very intelligent and gifted. Many of the older lamas marveled at his wisdom. He began to excel in the secular or public part of his education as well, but the maturing young lama was a lonely child. He spent hours in his room, gazing through the telescope that he had found in one of the storerooms.

Looking longingly out at the world far below the palace, he could see children running and playing. From time to time he would turn the telescope toward the nearby prison compound and watch the poor prisoners as they went about their lowly tasks. No doubt he felt a special closeness to them, since it sometimes must have seemed to him that he was in his own kind of prison.

Many times he begged to be allowed to visit his family and wished he could be like the boys he saw playing in the streets of Lhasa. As he matured, however, he came to understand that he was not like them. He had a special duty to his country and to his religion. He became more serious and dedicated to his education, but he never really outgrew his playful and curious

This young boy became the spiritual leader of Tibet in 1940; in another ten years, he assumed political leadership as well. (AP/Wide World Photos)

nature. Even in the most serious and dangerous times ahead, he maintained his good humor and remained curious about everything around him. People would marvel at his playful nature and his ability to joke even when his life and his country were being threatened.

Chapter 4

China "Liberates" Tibet

The background to the Chinese invasion of Tibet is complex. The two countries have long disagreed whether Tibet should be considered a part of China. For more than two hundred years, until the early twentieth century, Tibet was a part of the Chinese tributary system. In other words, Tibet made payments to the rulers of China in return for promises of protection from invaders. In 1720 the Qing (or Manchu) Dynasty in China sent armies to help the Tibetans defeat invading Mongol armies. The Qing established military camps in Tibet and installed two officers called *Ambos*. They said the Ambos were to help the Tibetans rule their homeland.

Then, in the early twentieth century, the British forcibly removed Tibet from China. Great Britain wanted to use Tibet as a buffer between their Indian empire and the Russians, who threatened in neighboring Afghanistan. In 1913, when the Qing Dynasty in China collapsed, the thirteenth Dalai Lama declared Tibet independent. The Chinese, however, never surrendered their claim that Tibet was a historical and essential part of China.

Furthermore, the fate of Tibet was tied to political events that occurred within China. From 1928 to 1949, China was ruled by the Nationalist government, led by Chiang Kai-shek. After the death of the thirteenth Dalai Lama in 1933, the leaders of Tibet found themselves increasingly coming under the control of this Chinese government. By the 1940's, however, the Nationalist government was weakening. Various Chinese warlords ruled large areas of Tibet during the chaotic years of World War II.

During World War II, Chinese Nationalist and Communist forces, normally fierce rivals, cooperated to help defeat Japan. After the war, in 1945, civil war broke out in China between the Nationalists and the increasingly powerful Communists. It lasted four years. In mid-1949, Chiang's government was losing the war against the Communist forces of Mao Zedong. The Tibetans tried to use the opportunity to regain their independence. In July of that year they forced all the Chinese out of Lhasa and hoped that they would not return.

Such hopes were short-lived, however. The Communists won the civil war and founded the People's Republic of China in October, 1949. Mao declared that his People's Liberation Army (PLA) would "liberate" Tibet and "restore it back to the Chinese Motherland." Tibet had only 3,500 soldiers in its tiny, ill-equipped, and badly trained army. They stood little chance against the battle-hardened and well-equipped 20,000 troops of the PLA.

Tibet Before the Invasion

Tibet was a sparsely populated and poor country. Until the late nineteenth century, it had long been mismanaged by a corrupt nobility and religious establishment. Then, during the reign of the thirteenth Dalai Lama, from 1876 to 1933, the country had been well governed. The people were free to farm their own plots of poor soil or tend their herds of animals in the foothills of the Himalayas.

During the early part of the fourteenth Dalai Lama's reign, however, many corrupt men took advantage of the fact that their new leader was only a child. They began to treat the peasants badly. Nearly 60 percent of the Tibetan people were tenants or sharecroppers who worked the land for rich nobles. Many of the Buddhist temples also owned large tracts of land. The poor peasants who worked on church lands were no better off than those who worked on land owned by the corrupt

34

nobles. Because nearly 15 percent of Tibetan males were monks, who did not grow the food they ate, there was an even greater burden placed on the peasants who did the work. In addition to these problems, civil war broke out in 1947 when two monasteries fought over who would control the young Dalai Lama.

Therefore, when the new Communist Chinese government promised to free the peasants from their crushing debts and to give more people a share of the land and wealth, some of the people were sympathetic. China was also quick to use the long history of bad feelings between the Kham people (Tibetans who lived in the mountains of eastern Tibet) and Tibetans who lived in the Lhasa valley. The Chinese promised the mountain people a larger share of Tibet's wealth and a greater voice in the government if they would support the People's Liberation Army. Ironically, six years later, the Kham would become rebellious and give the Chinese severe problems. In this early stage, however, they helped the PLA to conquer Tibet.

The PLA was careful to train their troops in the Tibetan language, religion, and customs so that when they approached and occupied areas of Tibet the lives of the people actually did improve for a while. In this early period, the PLA also tried to compromise to avoid bloodshed. It appeared to many people that Tibet really was being freed from its corrupt government.

The Boy Becomes a Man Before His Time

The People's Liberation Army invaded Tibet in October, 1950, and the Tibetan government appealed to the world for assistance against the invasion. No nation offered aid. Members of the government then decided that it might help if they named the young Dalai Lama the political leader of Tibet (he was already the country's religious leader). They hoped that the world would be more sympathetic to the pleas of a young monk than it had been to those of a corrupt government.

The Dalai Lama at age fifteen, shortly after the Chinese invasion of Tibet began.
(AP/Wide World Photos)

The fifteen-year-old boy was hurriedly installed as Tibet's political leader two years before the traditional age for the Dalai Lama to assume power.

Many people in the Tibetan government feared for the safety of the Dalai Lama. Although he wanted to stay with his people, it was decided by him, his family, and the top leaders of the government that they should flee to Yatung, along the border with Nepal. They left Lhasa in December, less than two months after the Dalai Lama became the country's leader. With them, for safekeeping, they took all the gold and silver they could move from the country's treasury. He later wrote, "to Tibetans, the person of the Dalai Lama is supremely precious, and whenever conflict came I had to allow my people to take far more care of me than I would have thought of taking of myself." Thousands of monks, fearing that the Dalai Lama would never return to Tibet, threw themselves in front of the horses of the fleeing party. The Dalai Lama finally convinced them that he would return soon, after the situation became less dangerous.

During this period the Dalai Lama began to experiment with the powers he had been given as king. He had ideas about how to redistribute farm and grazing lands so that the poor peasants could own their own land. He devised a plan to buy land from the rich nobles and temples using government bonds—basically, promises from the government to pay in the future. The land would then be sold to the poor people at reduced prices to be paid in small installments over many years.

He also tried to bring different kinds of people into the government in the hope of creating a more democratic leadership. He had been truly shocked when he discovered how badly the corrupt Tibetan leaders had been treating the people. Unfortunately, the young Dalai Lama never got to put these reforms into action in Tibet, because the Chinese would not allow it. Years later, however, when he was to form his government-in-exile in India, he would be able to put some of his ideas into practice.

While the newly crowned Dalai Lama waited in Yatung to hear responses to his pleas for help, the Chinese government forced a Tibetan delegation in Beijing, the capital of China, to sign an agreement. Known as the Seventeen-Point Agreement, it recognized that Tibet was part of China.

The Seventeen-Point Agreement

This agreement promised that although Tibet was to "rejoin" the Chinese "motherland," the Communists would protect Tibetan customs. China would respect the Buddhist religion, honor the Dalai Lama, and restore good, efficient government to the country. Basically, the Chinese promised that the people of Tibet would be allowed to remain independent in their lifestyles but not in their government.

The Chinese general in charge of the People's Liberation Army in the area came to Yatung, where he met the young Dalai Lama. The general offered him protection and assured him that Tibetans would be free to live their lives as before. Because he had received no support from any other nation, the Dalai Lama decided to return to Lhasa for the good of his people. He later wrote, "We were helpless. Without friends there was nothing else we could do but acquiesce, submit to the Chinese dictates in spite of our strong opposition, and swallow our resentment. We could only hope that the Chinese would keep their side of this one-sided bargain."

Captive in His Own Palace

After returning to Lhasa in August, 1951, the Dalai Lama soon found that he was nothing more than a figurehead in the new government and a prisoner in his own palace. The Chinese began a program of political and land reforms similar

---

First Six Points of the Seventeen-Point Agreement

1. The Tibetan people shall be united and drive out the imperialist agressive forces from Tibet; that the Tibetan people shall return to the big family of the motherland—the People's Republic of China.

2. The Local Government of Tibet shall actively assist the People's Liberation Army to enter Tibet and consolidate the national defenses.

3. In accordance with the policy toward nationalities laid down in the Common Program of the Chinese People's Political Consultative Conference, the Tibetan People have the right of exercising national regional autonomy under the unified leadership of the Central People's Government.

4. The Central Authorities [the Chinese government] will not alter the existing political system in Tibet. The Central Authorities also will not alter the established status, functions, and powers of the Dalai Lama. Officials of various ranks will hold office as usual.

5. The established status, functions, and powers of the Panchen Lama shall be maintained.

6. By the established status, functions, and powers of the Dalai Lama and Panchen Lama is meant the status, functions, and powers of the thirteenth Dalai Lama and the ninth Panchen Lama when they were in friendly and amicable relations with each other.

---

to those that they had already started in the rest of China. The most corrupt and oppressive nobles and lamas were imprisoned, and the entire nation underwent a process of "thought reform." In order to pretend that they still honored and respected the religion and customs of the country, the Chinese leaders allowed some lamas to continue their religious studies—but under the close watch of the People's Liberation Army. The Dalai Lama was appointed vice-chair of the government of the Chinese People's National Congress.

Despite appearances, however, the Dalai Lama had very little say in the new government of Tibet. The country itself was divided into three parts—to make it easier to govern, the

Chinese claimed. The Dalai Lama was not given much to do except attend and preside over endless committee discussions. The Chinese were careful to pack every government committee and office with PLA officers or with those Tibetans who were eager to cooperate with China.

The Dalai Lama also had very little personal freedom. The Chinese argued that "reactionary elements" (their term for anyone who did not cooperate with the PLA) might try to kill him; therefore, he must remain under their protection. In some ways the young king had been a prisoner in his own palace even before the Chinese came, because his every movement around the country caused tremendous disturbances. People would stop whatever they were doing and throw themselves on the ground in prayer. Now, however, he could not even greet his own people because of the PLA "protection" all around him.

A Trip to Beijing

In 1954 the nineteen-year-old Dalai Lama was invited to attend the National People's Conference in Beijing. The Tibetan people suspected that the Chinese were really kidnapping their young king. Thousands lined the road out of Lhasa to bid a tearful farewell. The Dalai Lama tried to assure them that he would return soon, but many feared they might never see him again.

The journey to Beijing took more than two months. The Chinese had only recently begun to build a road through the mountains, and much of the road was still under construction. The trip began in the 1931 Dodge that the Dalai Lama had tinkered with for so many years. Before long, however, they transferred to Chinese jeeps. Finally they had to travel on horseback. When the group finally reached Beijing, the Dalai Lama was paraded around in the company of China's most important leaders. They were eager to present a picture to the world that the Dalai Lama was being treated well. They hoped that the pictures of the young religious leader with China's most important people would convince the world that all was well in Tibet.

During this time the Dalai Lama was quite impressed with the ideals of Marxism, upon which Communist governments

The Dalai Lama (left) being greeted by Chairman Mao Zedong at the National People's Conference in Beijing, China. (AP/Wide World Photos)

claimed to base their economic systems. Marxism, based on the writings of Karl Marx, called for the sharing of wealth and power, the equality of all people, and the creation of a classless, democratic society. The Dalai Lama had been dismayed when he discovered that he had in many ways been a prisoner of the corrupt government in the Potala Palace. He now hoped that he could cooperate in improving the lives of his people.

He was impressed by the sincerity and good will of many Communist leaders in China. He was particularly impressed by the simplicity and earnestness of Chairman Mao Zedong. He later wrote of Mao, "I was convinced that he himself would never use force to convert Tibet into a Communist state." He took the advice of Mao and others who urged him to study Marxism during his six months in Beijing. He still had nagging doubts about the antireligious attitude of the Communists— Karl Marx had stated that religion was the opiate of the masses and should be abolished. Yet the Dalai Lama tried to keep an open mind.

Several incidents in Beijing, however, began to give him serious doubts about Chinese promises to maintain the Tibetan lifestyle. He had heard from his advisers that the People's Liberation Army back in Tibet had begun to round up and arrest "dissidents"—anyone who did not support their policies. When he asked Mao and other leaders about this, they first assured him that such policies were temporary, but then they began to threaten him.

At a banquet, the Dalai Lama showed Mao the Tibetan custom of throwing a pinch of cake up to the ceiling as if offering it to heaven and the Buddha. Mao joined in the fun, but he then threw a pinch on the ground, as if he were offering some to the devil as well. This shocked the Dalai Lama. It indicated to him that perhaps Mao and the Chinese were not as interested in preserving Tibetan religious customs as they claimed to be. He still was convinced, however, that the Chinese were serious about improving the lives of the Tibetan people. He had seen with his own eyes how hard the Chinese Communist Party was working to help their own poor. Surely, he thought, they would do the same for the Tibetan poor.

The Return to Tibet

The Dalai Lama returned to Lhasa in 1955. He was shocked to see the changes that had taken place in the many months that he had been gone. Hundreds of monks had been arrested and sent away to remote prisons, where many of them died. Former prisoners told of being tortured, beaten, raped, humiliated, and starved into submission. Horrified witnesses described mass graves of monks who had died in captivity.

Tibet had always been a poor country. The quality of its rocky soil was poor; it had a very high elevation and suffered from a lack of rainfall. Yet even during the very worst times of corrupt administrations, Tibet still had enough food for its people. In fact, there had always been a surplus of food because the farmers worked very hard and the country had a small population. Now, however, with the addition of thousands of PLA soldiers to feed—and with the often wasteful and inefficient uses of land by the Chinese—there began to be famine and malnutrition. The Tibetans, of course, suffered much more than did the Chinese who had taken power. It seemed to the Dalai Lama that the poor farmers had only exchanged one set of corrupt oppressors for another.

The peasants who had been promised title to their own land instead were rounded up and forced to work in communes that were little better than work camps. In order to make this farming work more efficient, according to the Chinese, men were separated from women, and children were taken from their parents and placed in youth camps. To conserve cooking fuel, everyone ate together in large kitchens instead of in smaller family groups. The Chinese rulers argued that it made much more sense to have one large cooking fire to feed a hundred than to have twenty smaller fires to feed the same number.

Because of this policy, families were split up. The Chinese felt that this would make it easier to control the children and educate them in the ideas of Marxism. It would also be easier to control the parents, because their children became hostages. Those who resisted or tried to escape were whipped, tortured, and denied food. Children were taken from their parents and sent to "education camps." They were taught that Tibetan customs and the Buddhist religion should be abolished because they were old-fashioned and corrupt. The Tibetan language was no longer taught in schools. Children who lapsed into their native tongue were severely punished. Worst of all, at least as far as the Dalai Lama was concerned, was the assault on the Buddhist religion by the Communists.

The Panchen Lama

Second only to the Dalai Lama in prestige in Tibet was the Panchen Lama. Like the Dalai Lama, he was believed to be a reincarnation of a bodhisattva and was therefore much revered and worshiped. He, like the Dalai Lama, had been born in the Chinese-governed northeast. The Chinese had controlled him for two years. In fact, before entering Tibet, the People's Liberation Army announced that the Panchen Lama had requested that Tibet be liberated. Two years younger than the Dalai Lama, he seemed to be more sympathetic to Marxism. He was among the Tibetans who were cooperating with the Chinese. Whether or not he actually agreed with the anti-Buddhist policies of the Chinese, most of those new policies were done in his name. Monks were forced to leave their temples and work as commoners in the communes. Often they were forced to give up their vows of celibacy and to marry former nuns.

People were no longer allowed to donate food for the monks to the temples. Many temples were closed and boarded up after their holy writings and other precious relics were removed. It was said that they were being placed in "safekeeping," but often the Buddhist statues were melted

44

down for their gold and silver. The precious metals were then taken out of the region to China. Many of Tibet's ancient treasures were sold to foreigners in Beijing antique shops.

Ten years later the religious community would come under even harsher attack during China's Great Proletarian Cultural Revolution, which lasted from 1966 to 1976. Even in this early phase, however, it was clear that the Communists wanted to destroy the power of the church. As conditions in Tibet worsened, it seemed to the people that the next target for the Chinese would be the Dalai Lama himself.

The Dalai Lama (left) and the Panchen Lama. (AP/Wide World Photos)

Chapter 5

The Flight to India

The Dalai Lama found himself in a very dangerous position after his return from Beijing in 1955. He hoped that by cooperating with China he could spare his people the worst aspects of occupation by a foreign army. He also still believed—at least partly—the promises of Mao and other Chinese leaders, such as Zhou Enlai and Deng Xiaoping. If only they really knew of the harsh way his people were being treated, he thought, there certainly would be changes.

Nehru's Invitation

Although he sent several letters to Mao, he could not be sure that they had even been delivered to him. He felt that he had to find a way to express his concerns. He needed to capture the attention of the leaders in some dramatic way.

The opportunity at last arose. The prime minister of India, Jawaharlal Nehru, invited both the Dalai Lama and the Panchen Lama to attend ceremonies marking the twenty-five-hundredth anniversary of the Buddha's death in India. At first the Chinese leaders denied them the right to go. After some public pressure from Nehru and other Asian leaders, however, the Chinese realized that unless they allowed these high lamas to go it might look like they were being held prisoners in their own land. Permission was granted and, in 1956, they left for India.

The Dalai Lama Comes of Age

The Dalai Lama was now twenty-two years old and considerably wiser after seven years of living under a Chinese

The Dalai Lama (center) arrives in India in 1956 for celebrations of Buddha's twenty-five-hundredth birthday. Seen here with Indian Prime Minister Nehru (left) and Indian Vice President Saravapalli Radhakrishnan. (AP/Wide World Photos)

Communist government. In the next few years he would show himself to be worthy of his nation's trust and honor.

As soon as he was safely away from Chinese control, he began to talk of asking for asylum in India. He thought that if he could criticize the Chinese treatment of his people while in India, it would embarrass China into changing its policies. Much to his surprise, however, Nehru was not enthusiastic about these plans. He lectured the Dalai Lama that the only way to work for reform was from the inside, not from the outside. He must return to Tibet and serve his people, Nehru said. Nehru also reminded him that India, like most other Asian nations, considered Tibet to be part of China and that India could not support Tibetan independence.

Part of the problem was that Nehru had his own serious problems with China. The world's two most populous nations were arguing about the border that separated them. Nehru did not want to anger the Chinese by supporting the Dalai Lama's claim that Tibet was independent.

More Chinese Promises

Despite these warnings from Nehru, the Dalai Lama hoped to use the threat of asylum to capture the attention of the Chinese leaders. Chinese foreign minister Zhou Enlai came to India to talk with the Dalai Lama. Zhou assured him that if mistakes had been made in the administration of reforms, China would investigate and then correct them. He told him that Mao had only that year promised that no real changes in the customs of Tibet would be made for years, perhaps decades. The Panchen Lama also suggested to the Dalai Lama that they both return to work for the improvement of conditions in Tibet. Many of the Dalai Lama's advisers thought that if he stayed in India the Chinese would be harsher in their treatment of the monks than they would be if he were in his homeland as a witness.

Whether or not the Dalai Lama really believed the Chinese government's new promises, he agreed to return to Tibet. His brothers, who had been reunited with him for the first time in many years, refused to return with him. His mother remained in India for another eighteen months because the Dalai Lama wanted her to be safe in case things went badly for the country. He returned to Lhasa in 1957.

1. The Dalai Lama receives a "tika," a traditional Hindu greeting, from an Indian girl. (AP/Wide World Photos)

2. The Dalai Lama, shown here in 1990, spends much time traveling and speaking on behalf of peace and Tibet's people. (AP/Wide World Photos)

3. The Dalai Lama presents a traditional scarf to Norway's ambassador to the United States. (AP/Wide World Photos)

4. Buddhist monks at demonstrations that turned violent in Lhasa in October, 1987.
   Many Tibetans were killed by Chinese soldiers during the disturbances. (AP/Wide
   World Photos)

5. After the October, 1987, demonstrations, the Dalai Lama leads a prayer meeting for
   those who died in the unrest. (AP/Wide World Photos)

6. The Dalai Lama in Vienna, Austria, in 1986. (AP/Wide World Photos)

7. Buddhist monks in Dharamsala, India, which has been the Dalai Lama's home since 1960. (Edwin Bernbaum)

8. The Dalai Lama listens to a question at one of the many meetings and conferences he has
attended throughout the world. (AP/Wide World Photos)

9. The huge Potala Palace in Tibet, in which the Dalai Lama lived between the ages of five and twenty-three. He later said that it was "not a nice place to live." (Edwin Bernbaum)

10. The Dalai Lama's temple in Dharamsala. (Edwin Bernbaum)

11. A statue of Buddha in the Dalai Lama's temple in Dharamsala. (Edwin Bernbaum)

12. The Tibetan Children's Village in Dharamsala, where about 1,500 children live and go to school. (Diane M. Lowe)

13. The Dalai Lama, in Rio de Janeiro for environmental meetings in 1992, blesses Roman Catholic Cardinal Eugenio Salles. (AP/Wide World Photos)

Returning to Lhasa for the Last Time

As when he had returned from Beijing in 1955, the Dalai Lama was absolutely shocked at the changes that had happened since he left. Many temples were shut down, and thousands of monks had simply disappeared. Almost all of the peasants were being forced to work in communes. The city of Lhasa seemed to be full of newly arrived Chinese immigrants, who were living in Tibetan homes. Worse, the price of food had skyrocketed and there was starvation in the countryside. It was clear that the Tibetan people would not put up with much more without resorting to an armed rebellion.

The Dalai Lama tried to cooperate with the occupation army leaders, but his heart was not in it. He felt that he had made a mistake in believing the Chinese promises. The best he could do, he thought, was to apply himself to his religious studies while he still could. He would also try to soften the harshest policies of the Chinese. During this time the Dalai Lama began taking a series of examinations at the hands of the best religious teachers in the country. He received a high degree in Buddhist studies in early 1959.

In the meantime, a guerrilla-type rebellion had sprung up in the eastern mountains of Kham. Thousands of nomadic tribesmen took up arms against the People's Liberation Army. Ironically, this was the region of Tibet that had cooperated with the PLA during the Chinese invasion of 1950. China demanded that the Dalai Lama end this rebellion. He tried to do so, because he feared that his peaceful mountain people would be slaughtered by the ferocious PLA. When the rebels refused to surrender, the Chinese demanded that the Dalai Lama send his personal delegation to talk with the rebels. The Dalai Lama warned that if he did so, the delegates would probably only join the rebellion. His prediction came true in 1958, and a large section of the eastern part of the country was in rebellion by early 1959.

By and large the rebellion was begun and continued by the nomadic tribal people in the region. The United States' Central Intelligence Agency (CIA) trained and supplied some rebel groups with arms and other supplies, but for the most part the courageous mountain people fought the better-armed Chinese army on their own. By the middle of 1958, thousands of the rebels had been killed or wounded. Many of the survivors began to flee to neighboring Nepal, Sikkim, and India.

A Standoff Outside the Palace

By 1959 it was clear that the Chinese government had absolutely no intention of keeping the promises that it had

The Dalai Lama (on the white horse) escaping over the Himalayas to India in 1959. (AP/ Wide World Photos)

made to the Dalai Lama in India. He later recalled in wonder, "They seem to lie without any shame. How is one to trust anything they say?"

In early March, 1959, the commander of the People's Liberation Army invited the Dalai Lama to attend a performance of a visiting dance troupe at the PLA camp outside Lhasa. The Dalai Lama was willing to do so until the commander requested that he leave his usual bodyguard of soldiers at home "so as not to stir up the people." Almost everyone believed that this was a trick to capture him and take him back to Beijing as a prisoner. That night a huge crowd of common people and monks surrounded the Norbulinga Palace and refused to allow anyone to enter or leave. They were determined to protect the Dalai Lama.

The Chinese commander was furious. He demanded that the people go away. Days went by, however, and the people refused to leave. The situation became increasingly tense and dangerous. When the crowd did not leave after a nearly week-long standoff, the commander had his soldiers fire two artillery shells into the crowd as a warning.

The Dalai Lama concluded that it was now time to flee. He had tried to negotiate a peaceful settlement to this confrontation, but he saw that his people were willing to fight and even risk death. Some in the crowd had become violent, and one of his own advisers had been mistakenly stoned by the crowd—they thought the poor man had come to take the Dalai Lama away. He decided that if he remained, the situation would probably grow even more dangerous and many might be killed.

On the night of March 17, 1959, he, his younger brother, his mother—who had only recently joined him in Tibet—and some of his closest advisers snuck out of the palace and began a harrowing two-week escape from the country.

Over the Mountains and Through the Woods

Even in this dangerous and tense time, the Dalai Lama thought to himself that the events of their escape seemed almost silly. Disguising himself as a Tibetan soldier, he slung an ancient rifle over his shoulder. He had to hide his distinctive eyeglasses; because he was one of the few Tibetans who wore glasses, they would have made him easily recognizable. Leaving the palace in the dead of night, he and his party stumbled around in pitch darkness. Finally, they linked up with bands of mountain rebels who escorted them high into the Himalayan Mountains on the journey to India.

Along the way they had to dodge scouts from the PLA as well as roving bands of Tibetan bandits who would strike at defenseless caravans. The tiny party had to depend upon the guerrilla units and the monasteries in the area for protection. They spent their nights at monasteries, and by day they traveled from one monastery to the next.

In one frightening moment high in the mountains, as they neared the border with Nepal, a plane flew overhead. The Dalai Lama thought that if he could see the plane, then the people in the plane (who were certainly Chinese) could probably see them against the snow that surrounded them. He urged his party to hurry even more in case they had been sighted. Their greatest fear was that the Chinese had spotted them from the air and were waiting to ambush them before they could cross the border out of Tibet.

After many days of hard travel, little sleep, and poor food, people in the party began to suffer from various illnesses. Especially troubling for these city dwellers from the Lhasa valley was the thin air of the high mountains. In the last days the Dalai Lama himself became very ill from dysentery. He had to be strapped onto the back of a yak for the final exhausting miles.

He was so weak and sick that he was unable to stand. The

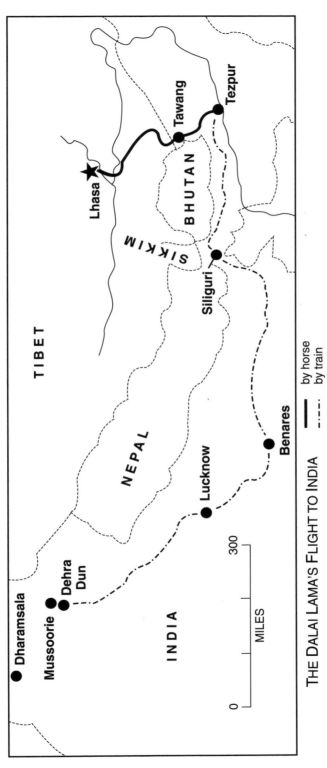

THE DALAI LAMA'S FLIGHT TO INDIA

by horse —————
by train —·—·—·—

temperature was so cold high in the mountains that the Dalai Lama's eyebrows froze (much to his later amusement). He rested in a peasant hut for a few days. Finally, on March 31, 1959, he and his party emerged from the woods into India. They were met by hundreds of worried people who had heard of his escape and had feared for his life. Reporters from many of the world's most important newspapers stood by, eager to ask questions. Hundreds of flashbulbs exploded as photographers captured the historic moment on film. The Dalai Lama was only three months shy of his twenty-fifth birthday. As he stepped out of the woods into freedom, he realized that the Tibetan part of his life was probably over and the difficult time of exile was just beginning.

Chapter 6

A Home Away from Home

The flight from his homeland had been a great adventure for the young Dalai Lama. For all of his life he had been so overprotected in his palaces that even his sickness and the dangers along the way added to the sense of high adventure. He later said that it seemed very much like playing soldiers back in the palace. Yet once he was safely away from the Chinese government, he realized that the excitement was over and the most difficult part of his life was ahead of him.

His first problem was how to feed and care for the hundreds of people who had made the journey with him. Also, within weeks, thousands more of his people escaped from Tibet and began to arrive in India. The Tibetan treasury, which had been brought out of the country nearly ten years before (when he had fled to Yatung), would only be enough to support him, his family, and his closest advisers. What could be done for the thousands of other Tibetans?

Another problem was that the Indian government of Nehru was still not enthusiastic about sheltering him. Nehru feared that this might threaten India's already shaky foreign relations with China. As had happened when the Dalai Lama first appealed for world aid in 1950, no other country seemed interested in recognizing Tibet's independence from China. After the first flush of interest by the world's journalists, the world turned its interest to other news and forgot about remote, isolated Tibet.

The Chinese government quickly imposed a news blackout, so the world did not hear that the PLA was slaughtering thousands of Tibetans. The PLA responded ferociously to the

Arrested Tibetan monks, after demonstrations in Lhasa, huddled in the back of a Chinese truck and guarded by armed Chinese troops. (AP/Wide World Photos)

rebellion. The poorly armed Tibetans were massacred before they could surrender.

The PLA did not hesitate to use artillery, even in the populated cities. Many villages that had helped the rebellion were entirely wiped out. Temples and monasteries that were suspected of harboring rebels were destroyed; everyone inside was killed. It may never be known how many Tibetans died. The Chinese army itself estimated (in a document captured by the Tibetan rebels) that more than eighty thousand Tibetans were killed. It was little wonder that thousands more fled the country with little more than the clothes on their backs. Hundreds, perhaps thousands of people died on the dangerous journey.

Feeding His Hungry People

The greatest immediate problem facing the Dalai Lama was feeding these thousands of Tibetan refugees who came stumbling out of the mountains. Many of the oldest and youngest who had fled did not survive the journey. The people who managed to escape alive desperately needed food, shelter, and medical attention. Many had suffered frostbite or other injuries along the way; others had been wounded by the PLA in the March, 1959, uprising. Still others had been robbed by bandits along the way.

Worse yet, many who had escaped unharmed quickly became ill in India from the intense heat, from diseases for which they had no natural immunities, or from lack of food. Something also had to be done quickly for the hundreds of orphans whose parents had died or disappeared along the way. Without someone to care for all of these refugees, many more would die.

The Indian government tried to do what it could. Young, healthy Tibetans were put into camps, where they worked on road construction in the mountains. The very young, the old, and the sick were placed in refugee camps, where they could be fed and receive medical care. The Dalai Lama expressed his appreciation for this help, but he realized that a better plan had to be made for the long-term care of his people. He did not know how long his people would have to stay in exile, nor did he have any idea how many more people would risk the dangerous journey, but he knew that he had to do something for them.

After a time he was able to convince Nehru and the Indian government that the work and refugee camps were not the best long-term arrangement for the Tibetans. India agreed to create settlements where the Tibetans could preserve their way of life. Unfortunately, since most of these settlements were in the hot southern part of India, the Tibetans suffered greatly from the intense heat. They also found it difficult to grow the same kinds of food that they had grown in Tibet. The yaks that had been not only their transportation but also their source of milk, butter, meat, and hair for clothing could not live in such a hot climate. Fortunately, there were many Tibetan merchant families who had lived in India for a long time. They helped their newly arrived cousins to adjust to their new surroundings.

With the help of "start-up money" provided from the Dalai Lama's personal wealth, several of these refugee settlements became self-supporting within a year. The Tibetans began to weave colorful sweaters, which they sold to tourists. By the end of that first year in exile, most of the Tibetans were at least clothed, well-fed, and able to practice their religion freely for the first time in over ten years.

A Refugee Government

Within days of his escape from Tibet, the Dalai Lama began to establish a government-in-exile. He hoped that if he could create a more democratic form of government while in exile, it would serve as a model for a new government when he and his people were allowed to return to Tibet. He had tried to do this ten years before, when he fled Tibet for the first time. When he had returned to Lhasa in 1951, he tried to reform the land ownership and social customs in the country, but the Chinese did not allow him to make changes. In addition, the conservative (and often corrupt) nobles and lamas who had been part of his government in Tibet had never favored land or political reforms.

Now, with time on his hands, he called his advisers together, along with many other Tibetans who had escaped. He asked everyone to give him their ideas about how a new government might be established. Within a year he had established an assembly to discuss and write a new

The twenty-three-year-old Dalai Lama addresses a gathering in Tezpur, North India. (AP/Wide World Photos)

constitution. A year later the assembly presented him with a constitution, but he was not satisfied. He asked them to make it even more democratic. There should be a section, he said, that would allow the people to depose and replace the Dalai Lama if they wished. Another section should make it possible for them to choose another type of leader if they desired.

He preferred that the people be able to elect their own leaders rather than have the Dalai Lama—or any other ruler—imposed upon them against their wills. The fact that most of the people who had escaped from Tibet were relatively young and liberal-minded made the creation of these reforms easier. Because the older, more conservative nobles and lamas among them were now cut off from their power and wealth back in Tibet, their influence was weakened.

The assembly elected men among themselves to act as political leaders and suggested a small voluntary tax to help pay for the government. Before long, all of the various refugee settlements were electing their own representatives to the government-in-exile. The Indian government was happy to see this development, because India called itself the "world's largest democracy." The Dalai Lama, too, was pleased, because this new form of government was humane and democratic.

The most positive reform, as the Dalai Lama saw it, was the establishment of a network of free public schools for young Tibetans. The Indian government provided many teachers for the Tibetan communities. Although the Dalai Lama was grateful, he wanted the schools to be Tibetan, not Indian. He wanted his people to be educated in their own language, history, religion, and culture. He asked all of his advisers to take some time from their other duties to help teach the Tibetan language to older students. In turn, the older ones would teach the younger children.

Before long the Tibetans themselves were teaching their children as well as teaching their language to some of the Indian teachers who had come to help. Even older people who had never learned to read or write back in Tibet were being educated. The Dalai Lama stressed that the most important

The Dalai Lama giving darshan, a type of blessing, to followers not long after arriving in Mussoorie, India, in 1959. (AP/Wide World Photos)

thing people could do to work for the independence of Tibet was to educate themselves and their children.

The Dalai Lama knew that this younger group of educated Tibetans would help to make his government-in-exile more democratic and international in outlook. He would even joke that perhaps the Chinese had done them a favor by shocking them out of their inward-looking attitudes.

Appeals to the World: Is Anyone Listening?

Unfortunately, even as these important educational and political reforms were taking place, the government-in-exile was not having much luck attracting support from the rest of the world.

Even while he was on the road fleeing Tibet in 1959, the Dalai Lama had appealed to the world. In his first news conference with the reporters who awaited him at the Indian border, he asked for aid. The rest of the world, however, was not particularly interested in the plight of 100,000 Tibetan refugees. International tensions were high in the early 1960's, and Tibet was a distant land with no military or economic importance.

The Cold War, a struggle between the United States and the Soviet Union for world influence and control, was at its height. The Cuban Missile Crisis of 1962 brought the threat of nuclear war to the forefront of world concerns. Many African nations were fighting to liberate themselves from the control of their European colonial masters. Even worse, in 1962, China invaded India over a border dispute. This made the Tibetans' problem a very minor one as far as the United Nations was concerned. The U.N. had passed a resolution in October, 1959, condemning the human rights abuses by the Chinese in Tibet, but it offered no opinion as to the Tibetans' claims of independence.

Even India refused to recognize the independence of Tibet.

It continued to provide asylum for the Dalai Lama and his people, but it asked them not to become involved in any political actions. The Dalai Lama obeyed and tried not to create problems for his Indian hosts.

Chapter 7

The World Traveler

China and India ended their war and settled their border dispute in 1962. In 1964, Indian Prime Minister Nehru died. After these events, the Dalai Lama began to reach out to the world community more. He had been studying the English language for some time, and he finally felt confident enough to accept invitations to go abroad. First he traveled to Buddhist countries, such as Thailand and Japan, then to other nations as well.

He was careful not to create political problems for his hosts, preferring to lecture on Buddhist topics. As time went on, however, and his confidence at public speaking increased, he slowly began to speak more openly about the problems of his exiled people. Because India and China had settled their dispute, the Indian government was no longer so insistent that the Dalai Lama remain nonpolitical.

Genocide in Tibet

The 1960's were terrible years for the people still in Tibet. The uprising of March, 1959, had been suppressed harshly by the Chinese. Estimates of the number of Tibetans killed are as high as 100,000. Captured Chinese army documents put the number at a minimum of 87,000 killed in battles alone. Thousands more were arrested and simply thrown into prison for years. There they were starved and tortured; many were executed. Even thousands of Tibetans who were not arrested were treated horribly.

Then, in 1966, the government of China began a program known as the Great Proletarian Cultural Revolution. Under

Mao Zedong's leadership, the Cultural Revolution sought to revitalize communism and root out "reactionaries" unwilling to devote themselves totally to Communist doctrine. Hordes of young people, known as Red Guards, were unleashed by Mao

In New York City on March 10, 1988, Tibetans and their supporters marched to the United Nations to protest China's policies. (AP/Wide World Photos)

to further the Cultural Revolution. Filled with revolutionary fervor, the Red Guard swept through all of China, causing violence and death. In Tibet, thousands of Tibetans, especially monks, were brutalized by the Red Guard. Almost all of Tibet's remaining hundreds of temples were looted, burned, or otherwise destroyed.

During this time China was determined to exterminate what it called the "feudal and corrupt" Tibetan culture. Very young children were kidnapped from their parents and sent to schools in China, where they were taught to hate their own native culture. The teaching of the Tibetan language and the practice of the Buddhist religion were both made illegal. The punishment for even keeping pictures of the Dalai Lama was death.

Yet the Tibetans refused to surrender to the oppression and genocide (racial or cultural murder) that they faced. The people continued to practice their religion quietly and privately. Every scrap of Buddhist sutra, every tiny piece of Buddhist relic, carving, sculpture, or painting, was treasured. Many thousands of these tiny scraps and pieces were hidden away or smuggled out of Tibet to India, where the Dalai Lama and his people collected them. They put them in the new temples they built there to preserve their culture.

High in the mountains, guerrilla soldiers continued their desperate fight against the Chinese. Although the Dalai Lama would have preferred nonviolent means of resistance, these brave rebels continued to fight despite the impossible odds. At first the United States, through the CIA, secretly assisted the guerrillas. After China and the United States established diplomatic relations in the early 1970's, however, this assistance stopped.

As the rest of the world went about its business, uncounted numbers of Tibetans—perhaps more than a million, or about 15 percent of the country's total population—lost their lives in this holocaust.

Conditions in Tibet Seem to Improve

After the deaths of Chinese leaders Mao and Zhou in 1976, the situation in Tibet brightened briefly. Mao's successor, Hua Guafeng, visited Tibet and was horrified at the poor conditions there. Most of the Chinese leaders in Tibet were recalled to China, and new people were sent to replace them. Hua and the Chinese government promised to end the genocide and began to invite the Dalai Lama publicly to return to Tibet.

As much as the Dalai Lama missed Tibet and longed to return, he knew that he could not do so until the Chinese had left. He had tried to work with the Chinese while in Tibet from 1951 to 1959, and he would not make that mistake again. He understood the old Tibetan proverb: "A prisoner criticizes his jailers only after being released from prison." Only if he remained free from Chinese control would he have influence and power. He insisted that if China wished to "settle the Tibetan question," they must make the reforms before he returned.

The Chinese government seemed to be sincere in its intentions. It began to improve conditions in Tibet. A few temples were rebuilt, and a few hundred monks were coaxed into returning to help rebuild others. In 1978, most political prisoners were released, including thirty-four former members of the Dalai Lama's 1959 government. The Tibetan language was once again taught in schools. People were once again allowed to farm their own pieces of land, and thousands were released from communes and work camps. Taxes were lowered, and in the very poorest areas they were actually abolished. Families were reunited, in some cases for the first time in fifteen years. Children were allowed to live at home instead of in boarding schools.

In 1978 the Panchen Lama was finally released from prison after ten years. He had been jailed for refusing to denounce the Dalai Lama. An invitation to the Dalai Lama to visit Tibet was made in his name. At last China "opened" Tibet to foreign visitors and invited the Dalai Lama to return to visit if he liked. Although the Dalai Lama refused to leave his exile, he agreed to send delegations from his government to inspect conditions in Tibet.

The Dalai Lama's Siblings Visit Tibet

The Dalai Lama sent a five-person delegation, led by his older brother Lobsang Samten, to visit Tibet in August, 1979.

The Chinese rulers warned the Tibetan people that if they approached the delegation they would be arrested. In spite of this, the delegation was swarmed by thousands of weeping Tibetans who kneeled around them asking for news of the Dalai Lama.

If the Chinese thought that the visitors would be impressed by what they saw in Tibet, they were very mistaken. The delegation was horrified at the poverty of the people and at the sight of hundreds of destroyed temples. In 1959 there had been 2,711 temples and monasteries in Tibet and some 120,000 monks. In 1979 there were only nine monasteries which had survived Chinese destruction; there were reported to be only 280 monks left.

The Dalai Lama's delegates were careful not to criticize the Chinese while in Tibet, but when they returned to report to the Dalai Lama, they told him of every horrible detail. Since he hoped that he could encourage China to make further improvements and reforms, he refused to voice his criticisms in public. However, he did criticize the Chinese privately in a secret discussion with them. They promised that reforms were quickly being implemented.

A year later—in May, 1980—he dispatched two more delegations to Tibet, one led by his older sister. Both of these delegations returned greatly displeased by the lack of new reforms in Tibet. It became apparent to the Dalai Lama that private criticisms would not work. At last he began to voice his displeasure in public. China was angered by his criticism, and negotiations for more visits were broken off.

Chinese Immigration and Environmental Destruction

After China's first few promising steps toward improvement, the situation in Tibet worsened again. China was embarrassed at the criticism voiced by the Dalai Lama, by

other exiled Tibetans, and by foreign visitors. The Chinese
tightened up restrictions for people who wished to visit Tibet.
They insisted that if the Dalai Lama wanted to improve
relations, then he should himself come to visit.

As much as he wished to go, he feared that if he did, the
Chinese would never let him leave. Their treatment of the
Panchen Lama and their continued broken promises made the
danger of his capture very real. It would be better to remain on
the outside to criticize and to remind the world of Tibet's
horror, he thought.

The Chinese government began a new tactic of "washing
out" the Tibetans by immigration. Thousands and then
millions of Chinese were promised money and land if they
would immigrate to Tibet. Soon Tibetans were becoming a
minority in their own land.

The Chinese ravaged the countryside in search of wealth to
support China's modernization. Coal, iron ore, and other
minerals were mined and exported to China; Tibet's forests
were leveled, and the wood was whisked out of the country.
The Chinese methods of "clear-cutting" (cutting down
everything, even the smallest, youngest trees) and failure to
replant trees in the forests left the area ravaged by erosion.
New crops were introduced into the country, some of which
leeched the minerals and nutrients out of the soil in just a few
harvests. Crops, when harvested, were sent out of the country.
Even Tibet's native food staple, barley, was exported to China.

Demonstrations and Death

In 1987, when the Dalai Lama was visiting the United
States, a group of monks tried to demonstrate peacefully in
Lhasa. The demonstration was put down brutally. Hundreds of
Tibetans were killed or wounded, and thousands more were
arrested. It became more and more apparent that China did not
intend to keep any prior promises of reform. In partial

response, on December 22, 1987, the government of the United States passed a bill condemning the most recent Chinese human rights abuses in Tibet.

Yet the United States was sending a mixed message to Beijing. Earlier in December, President Ronald Reagan had refused to receive the Dalai Lama during his visit to Washington, D.C. The Dalai Lama had been there to speak before the Joint Human Rights Committee of Congress. The United States was not alone: No other country in the world officially recognized the government-in-exile of the Dalai Lama.

Chinese People's Liberation Army soldiers guard a post office in Lhasa after demonstrations in March, 1989, turned violent. (AP/Wide World Photos)

Three months later, in March, 1988, a demonstration was held in Lhasa to mark the twenty-ninth anniversary of the Dalai Lama's flight from Tibet to India. It too was brutally squashed by the PLA. Martial law was declared by China, and the few newly restored civil rights were suspended once again.

Hundreds of Tibetans were arrested, tortured, and held without trial. On this occasion, the world became instantly aware of the repression, because many American, British, and Australian tourists happened to be in Lhasa at the time. They told their stories and showed their pictures of the harsh suppression to the news media.

A year later, on March 5, 1989, another peaceful demonstration was quickly put down in Lhasa. This brutal suppression of Tibetans was a dark omen. Three months later, pro-democracy demonstrations by Chinese students in Beijing's Tiananmen Square resulted in a massacre of students by the army. As the world recoiled in horror from the brutality of the Chinese government toward its own people, the Dalai Lama reminded everyone that China had been doing the same thing to his people for thirty years.

In December of 1989, the Dalai Lama was rewarded for his patience and for his insistence on nonviolence by being awarded the Nobel Peace Prize. When the people of Lhasa heard the news, they rejoiced in the streets. The captive population braved certain arrest, torture, and even death to celebrate. Thousands of people, old and young, stood silently in the shadow of the Dalai Lama's Potala Palace, tears of joy streaming down their faces. Red-robed monks, no longer able to contain their joy, shouted "Long live the Dalai Lama! Tibet for Tibetans!"

Moments later, the Chinese police waded into the peaceful crowd, then opened fire with automatic rifles. Hundreds of Tibetans were killed or wounded, and thousands more were rounded up like cattle and whisked away to the torture chambers of remote prisons.

The Dalai Lama in the 1990's

In the years since 1989, the Chinese government has continued to insist that Tibet is a part of China and has refused to discuss the possibility of its independence. From time to time they invite the Dalai Lama to come home. However, they make it clear that if he does so, he would live in Beijing, not in Lhasa. For his part, the Dalai Lama continues to work peacefully for a nonviolent solution to the Tibetan dilemma.

The governments of the world have refused to do much about Tibet except occasionally to condemn the latest abuses of human rights by China. American President George Bush, for example, perhaps fearing a break in diplomatic or trade relations with China, refused to meet publicly with the Dalai Lama. The United Nations continued to call on China to "solve the matter of Tibet peacefully." It is not likely to do more, however. Because the People's Republic of China sits on the U.N. Security Council, it could veto even a vote by the General Assembly. The U.N. is therefore unlikely to spring to Tibet's defense, as it did for invaded Korea in 1950 and Kuwait in 1991.

On the other hand, private organizations such as Asia Watch, Greenpeace, and Amnesty International have, from time to time, championed the cause of the Dalai Lama and Tibet. In addition, various environmental groups have responded to his calls for "universal responsibility" and for the establishment of the world's first "biosphere" in Tibet by inviting him to speak before their groups. He participated in the world's first environmental conference, organized by the United Nations, in Rio de Janeiro, Brazil, in the summer of 1992.

The American news media took up the Dalai Lama's cause in the early 1990's. Bill Moyers of the Public Broadcasting Service (PBS) narrated an hour-long television interview and documentary. Dan Rather did a similar interview for the Columbia Broadcasting System (CBS), and the "National Geographic Explorer" television series featured a segment on the Dalai Lama. National Public Radio (NPR) also has devoted a number of reports and interviews to the Dalai Lama and Tibet. Newspapers and magazines continue to raise the issue from time to time. Tibet's situation was discussed, for example, when the United States Congress debated granting "most-favored nation" trading status to China in 1991 and 1992.

As the Soviet Union, Yugoslavia, Czechoslovakia, and other former Communist states disintegrated into ethnic and religious wars in the early 1990's, and as the United Nations sprang to the aid of Kuwait in 1991, the world's attention was again torn away from Tibet and the Dalai Lama. Yet as long as the Dalai Lama lives, he continues to be a source of embarrassment for China. His nonviolent campaign for peace and freedom for his people continues to be a thorn in the side of Tibet's Chinese invaders.

Chapter 8

The Dalai Lama's Legacy of Peace

For more than thirty years, the Dalai Lama and thousands of his people have been in exile from their homeland. In his absence, more than a million Tibetans have died at the hands of their Chinese occupiers. Yet despite his grief over the crimes committed against his people, the Dalai Lama has continued to preach the gospel of love and nonviolence. He has continued to remind his people—and the world—that although China has been "cruel, unreasonable, inhumane, and illogical . . . I have absolutely no hatred in my heart for the Chinese people."

Through it all, he has gained the admiration of the world for his beliefs. Twenty years after his flight from Tibet, even the Soviet Union and other Communist countries called on their brothers in China to settle their dispute with this holy man and the people of Tibet. Thirty years after his exile began, the whole world recognized how unique this Buddhist monk was when the Nobel Peace Prize was awarded to him in December, 1989.

In the Nobel Prize ceremonies in Oslo, Norway, Egil Aarvik, the chair of the Nobel Peace Prize Committee, suggested that "it would be difficult to cite any historical example of a minority's struggle to secure its rights in which a more conciliatory attitude to the adversary has been adopted than in the case of the Dalai Lama. It would be natural to compare him with Mahatma Gandhi, one of this century's greatest protagonists of peace."

In the years since the Nobel Prize was granted to him, the Dalai Lama has continued to live quietly high in the foothills of India. He remains separated from his homeland by the Himalayan Mountains. He continues to travel and to preach peace, love, nonviolence, and what he calls "universal responsibility": the idea that all living beings are responsible for one another's happiness and well-being.

To be sure, he still calls for the liberation of Tibet. He has said: "Tibetans are entitled to all the rights that other free peoples have, including the preservation of their separate, unique identity and way of life. . . . The people must have the freedom to express themselves without fear." By 1987, however, he had changed his demands for complete and total independence of Tibet from Chinese control.

On December 10, 1989, the Dalai Lama received the Nobel Peace Prize from Egil Aarvik, chair of the Nobel Committee. (AP/Wide World Photos)

The World's First Zone of Ahimsa

Beginning in 1987, the Dalai Lama began to suggest to China that Tibetans would accept something less than total and complete independence. In a series of speeches to the United States Congress, he said that a new type of settlement might be negotiated, under United Nations protection.

Under such an agreement, China would leave Tibetan domestic politics to the Tibetans themselves but could continue to control Tibet's foreign affairs. Perhaps a federation something like the British Commonwealth could work as well for Tibet as it does for Canada, Australia, and New Zealand. He said, "Whether Tibet was independent or not doesn't matter so long as our people are happy. The fact that at the present moment our people are not happy is also more important than history."

In a speech to the European Parliament in Strasbourg, France, on June 15, 1988, he suggested a Five-Point Peace Plan for such a settlement:

1. Transformation of the whole of Tibet, including the eastern provinces of Kham and Amdo, into a Zone of Ahimsa, or nonviolence.
2. Abandonment of China's population transfer policy.
3. Respect for the Tibetan people's fundamental human rights and democratic freedoms.
4. Restoration and protection of Tibet's natural environment.
5. Commencement of earnest negotiations on the future status of Tibet and of relations between the Tibetan and Chinese peoples.

The key elements of his Zone of Ahimsa include demilitarizing the entire Tibetan plateau; prohibiting the manufacture and testing of nuclear weapons in Tibet; prohibiting nuclear power and other technologies that produce hazardous waste;

establishing international and regional organizations to promote peace and protect human rights; establishing programs to preserve resources and to protect all forms of life; and creating the world's first "biosphere," or natural park, to protect wildlife and plant life.

In other words, the Dalai Lama suggests that Tibet become a model for a new kind of political, social, and environmental cooperation in the world.

Peace for Tibet?

The Dalai Lama has been called both a visionary and a dreamer, but it could also be argued that he is a supreme realist. Before he developed his peace plan, he thoroughly analyzed the reasons the Chinese took Tibet in 1950. He realized that they could not simply surrender it, so he changed his mind about demanding complete independence. The new emphasis was on cooperation for mutual benefit. He suggested a number of reasons why his plan for a Zone of Ahimsa is the only type of idea that could work for both Chinese and Tibetans.

First, the Dalai Lama realized, China is seriously overpopulated and desperately needs more land. Tibet is one of the least populated areas of the world. However, its very high elevation, poor soil, and lack of rainfall make it difficult for the land to feed more people than it already does. New, nondestructive kinds of agriculture would have to be introduced in order for Tibet to grow enough food to help China feed its billion people. The Dalai Lama has proposed that agricultural cooperatives be set up to help solve Tibet's and China's food problems. Perhaps Tibet could begin growing new types of crops, with Chinese help, and exchange the food for goods manufactured in China.

Second, Tibet is rich in mineral and timber resources. The Dalai Lama is willing to share these with China, as long as the

Tibetan environment is not seriously damaged. The Chinese policies of clear-cutting the forests and using wasteful mining techniques, however, would have to be stopped. These methods have caused many problems, including severe erosion of Tibetan soil. New cooperation between Tibet and China might work toward Tibet's benefit: China could help provide Tibet with trade and access to the rest of the world. As the Dalai Lama has said, "We have no sea route. We are

The Dalai Lama with American singer John Denver (center) at the Earth Summit conference on the environment in Rio de Janeiro, Brazil, in 1992. (AP/Wide World Photos)

inaccessible because we live at such a high altitude. We are rich only in minerals, and you can't eat minerals."

Third, if Tibet were to become a Zone of Ahimsa, it could help both China and India feel more secure about their borders.

China views Tibet as a buffer between itself and India. If Tibet became a nonmilitary zone of peace, neither country would have to worry so much about the other and could save the money they spend keeping troops along the border.

Fourth, the Dalai Lama saw the political reasons that China could not grant independence to Tibet. If Tibet were to become independent, the other minority peoples in China might clamor for the same right. China could never grant independence to Chinese Turkestan, Mongolia, or Manchuria, because this would seriously damage China's prestige and power in the world. Through the creation of a Zone of Ahimsa, the Dalai Lama suggested, Tibet could remain part of the Chinese commonwealth: "If the Chinese follow their words with actions, if we Tibetans derive more benefit by remaining a member of the [Chinese] community, I would be willing."

The Future of the Dalai Lama

The future of Tibet remains very much in doubt. The future of the Dalai Lama himself is a different question, and it is a question that he has been asked many times. It is actually a twofold question, because the Dalai Lama is believed by Tibetans to be both one man named Tenzin Gyatso and the repeated reincarnation of the previous thirteen Dalai Lamas. Asked about the future of the institution of the Dalai Lama, he has said:

> The Dalai Lama came to be an important leader for Tibet, but that is not permanent. If that usefulness disappears, then it is not necessary to preserve the institution of the Dalai Lama. The issue of Tibet is not a problem with the Dalai Lama; it concerns the Tibetan people. It is possible that I am the last Dalai Lama.

As for himself, if the Tibetan people were to decide to have another type of leader, the Dalai Lama would gladly and peacefully retire. If the problems between China and Tibet were to be solved, he would very much like to live the life of a humble monk. He would welcome the opportunity to relax and pursue his religious studies—and perhaps even to tinker with clocks to his heart's content.

The Dalai Lama's legacy will forever be tied to the exile and genocide of the Tibetan people. He was thrust into the world's spotlight by events: the Chinese invasion of Tibet in 1950 and his own flight to India in 1959. His greatness has come from the way that he has handled himself. He has refused to become bitter, resentful, or vengeful. Instead, he has remained true to his religious faith and his Tibetan heritage. He has remained a peaceful symbol of the Tibetan national spirit to his people and has become a model for the rest of the world.

In a world filled with violence and hate, he represents the ideal peaceful soul. In a world that seems to be in danger of committing environmental suicide, he is a model for "universal responsibility." He might even be seen as the ultimate environmentalist. In a world where greed and envy sometimes seem to rule people's lives, he has created a model of the simple man. His message is clear: Live simply, love humanity. His legacy is perhaps best expressed in the words of Egil Aarvik's Nobel Prize presentation address:

> The message of Your Holiness, as we are hearing it, is avoid violence, work for negotiated peaceful settlements, seek change without bloodshed, freedom without anarchy, express national pride without nationalistic feeling. From the ancient and venerable Buddhist tradition, you bring us the message of the importance of seeing mind and matter, humanity and nature as one. From the great wisdom of the past comes guidance for our common future.

The Dalai Lama concluded his Nobel lecture on December 11, 1989, with a short prayer:

> *For as long as space endures,*
> *And for as long as living beings remain,*
> *Until then may I, too, abide*
> *To dispel the misery of the world.*

Books by the Dalai Lama

The Buddhism of Tibet and the Key to the Middle Way. New York: Harper & Row, 1975. As its title implies, this book is primarily a discussion of Tibetan Buddhism, but it also contains some information regarding the Dalai Lama's actions in the period after his first autobiography was published in 1962.

Freedom in Exile. New York: HarperCollins, 1990. The Dalai Lama's long-awaited update of his 1962 autobiography. Covers much of the same information found in *My Land and My People*. Written in a simple, readable style. Good illustrations.

My Land and My People. New York: McGraw-Hill, 1962. A moving autobiography in which the Dalai Lama explains his actions and his philosophy of nonviolence. Written in a simple, readable style. Not as complete as his later book *Freedom in Exile*, but more thorough in dealing with his early life.

Time Line

1935   *July 6.* The Dalai Lama is born Lhamo Dhondrub in Taktser, Tibet.

1937   *July.* The Dalai Lama is "discovered" in Taktser.

1939   *October 8.* The Dalai Lama arrives in Lhasa.

1940   *February 22.* The Dalai Lama is enthroned at the Potala Palace.

1947   *April.* Civil war breaks out in Tibet between rival monasteries over who will control the regency of the Dalai Lama.

1950   *October 7.* The invasion of Tibet by China's PLA begins.

1950   *November 7.* Tibet appeals to the United Nations for help.

1950   *November 17.* The Dalai Lama is installed as Tibet's secular leader.

1950   *December.* The Dalai Lama flees to Yatung.

1951   *May 23.* The Seventeen-Point Agreement between China and Tibet is signed.

1951   *August 17.* The Dalai Lama leaves Yatung to return to Lhasa.

1951   *October 24.* In a telegram to Mao Zedong, the Dalai Lama accepts the Seventeen-Point Agreement.

1954   *July 11.* The Dalai Lama leaves Lhasa for Beijing.

1954   *September 16.* The Dalai Lama arrives in Beijing to attend the National People's Congress.

1955   *Autumn.* Rebellion begins in Kham.

1956   *November 25.* The Dalai and Panchen lamas arrive in New Delhi to observe the twenty-fifth centenary of the death of Buddha.

1959   *March 1.* The Dalai Lama passes his *Geshe Lharampa*, or doctor of metaphysics examinations.

1959   *March 9.* Chinese authorities invite the Dalai Lama to come alone to a Chinese army camp, but the Tibetan people refuse to let him go.

1959   *March 17.* The Dalai Lama escapes from Lhasa; on March 31, he is granted political asylum in India.

1959   *April 24.* The Dalai Lama meets Jawaharlal Nehru in Mussoorie.

1959	*June 20.* The Dalai Lama denounces the Seventeen-Point Agreement.
1959	*October.* The United Nations votes to support Tibet against the Chinese invasion.
1960	*April.* The Dalai Lama moves from Mussoorie to Dharamsala.
1960	*August.* The International Commission of Jurists finds China in violation of sixteen articles of the Universal Declaration of Human Rights and guilty of genocide.
1960	*September 2.* The Commission of Tibetan People's Deputies is appointed.
1963	*March 4.* The provisional constitution of the Tibetan government-in-exile is published.
1978	*February 25.* The Panchen Lama is released after a decade of imprisonment.
1978	*November.* Thirty-four former members of the Dalai Lama's government are released after twenty years of imprisonment.
1979	*June 12.* The Dalai Lama visits the Soviet Union.
1979	*August 2.* A delegation of five members of the Tibetan government-in-exile is allowed to visit Tibet.
1980	*May.* The second and third delegations leave for Tibet.
1982	*April.* A three-member negotiating delegation visits Beijing; Chinese leaders invite the Dalai Lama to return but not to live in Tibet.
1983	*January.* China begins a new colonization campaign in Tibet.
1985	*July.* Ninety-one members of the U.S. Congress sign a letter to China urging direct talks with the Dalai Lama.
1985	*September.* The Dalai Lama's brother Lobsang Samten dies.
1987	*September.* The Dalai Lama announces his Five-Point Peace Plan at the Human Rights Caucus of the U.S. Congress; the next day, Congress passes a resolution in favor of the plan.
1987	*September-October.* Demonstrations in Lhasa are brutally suppressed by the Chinese; thousands are arrested, hundreds killed.
1987	*December 22.* U.S. President Reagan signs a bill condemning Chinese human rights abuses in Tibet.

1988	*March 5.* The *Monlam* festival results in more repression in Lhasa.
1988	*June 15.* The Dalai Lama presents his Five-Point Peace Plan, a new offer of shared governance for Tibet, at the European Parliament in Strasbourg.
1988	*Autumn.* China requests direct negotiations with the Tibetan government-in-exile; within six months, however, plans for negotiations stall.
1989	*January 28.* The Panchen Lama dies in Beijing.
1989	*March.* Thousands are arrested, hundreds killed, in demonstrations in Lhasa; martial law is imposed.
1989	*October 5.* The Nobel Peace Prize Committee announces that the Dalai Lama is the 1989 winner.
1989	*December 10.* The Dalai Lama is awarded the Nobel Peace Prize in Oslo, Norway; a week of demonstrations begins in Lhasa, at which many Tibetans are arrested.

Glossary

Ahimsa: The ancient Indian idea of "nonharming," employed by Mahatma Gandhi in his philosophy of "aggressive nonviolence"; the Dalai Lama wishes to establish a Zone of Ahimsa in Tibet.

Amdo: The northeastern province of Tibet, now officially part of Xinjiang Province of China.

Asylum: A refuge; in politics, "granting asylum" is allowing a person or group to stay in a place without fear of being expelled or persecuted.

Austin: A British-made car.

Avalokiteshvara: The Buddha of Mercy, who lived about 2,500 years ago; Tibetan Buddhists believe that the Dalai Lama is his "manifestation"; also called Chenrezig in Tibet.

Beijing: The capital city of China; also written Peking.

Bodhisattva: A Buddhist saint; a person who has reached the point of salvation, or enlightenment, but remains among humans to help them.

Buddhism: The major religion of Tibet as well as of many other areas of Asia; based on the ancient teachings of Siddhrtha Gautama (the Buddha), it emphasizes self-purification as the path to enlightenment.

Chamdo: Formerly an eastern province of Tibet, now incorporated with Amdo into Xinjiang and Sichuan provinces in China.

Chenrezig: See **Avalokiteshvara.**

Chiang Kai-shek: Nationalist Chinese leader; he was the leader of China from 1928 until 1949, when Mao Zedong established the People's Republic of China.

Communes: In Communist China, work camps where farmers were forced to live and work cooperatively.

Cuban Missile Crisis: A tense standoff between the United States and the Soviet Union in 1962, during which many people feared that a nuclear war would start; the Soviet Union was placing nuclear missiles in Cuba, and the U.S. demanded they be removed.

Dalai Lama: The person believed in Tibet to be the reincarnation of previous Dalai Lamas and a manifestation of the saint Avalokiteshvara; *Dalai* means "ocean," and *Lama* means "teacher."

Deng Xiaoping: The leader of the People's Republic of China who succeeded Hua Guafeng; sometimes written Teng Hsiao-p'ing.

Dharamsala: A city in northwest India; it has become the capital of the Dalai Lama's Tibetan government-in-exile.

Gandhi, "Mahatma" Mohandas K.: A great religious leader in India in the first half of the twentieth century; using nonviolent methods, he pushed for the independence of India from British rule (the title Mahatma means "great soul").

Genocide: The destruction of a religious, racial, or ethnic group, often carried out through murdering huge numbers of people.

Himalayan Mountains: The highest mountains in the world, located between China and India; the nations of Nepal, Sikkim, Bhutan, and Tibet all are located in the Himalayan foothills.

Hua Guafeng: The successor to Chinese Communist leader Mao Zedong; he came to power in 1976.

Great Proletarian Cultural Revolution: Often simply called the Cultural Revolution, it was Mao Zedong's attempt to rid China of "old customs, ᵃ it lasted from 1966 to 1976.

Ⱪ᜶ ᜶ ᜶ eastern Tibet who have carried on a guerrilla ᜶ ᜶ 1955.

᜶ three-year retreat; the
ɩ like an Indian

ɔ 1976; he defeated
's Republic of China.
Karl Marx
.; Marx believed that
system was needed.
Jia; he served from 1947

ɩnd India.
the Nobel Foundation to
ɩce; the Nobel Prizes were
Jobel of Sweden.

Nomaɔɔ. ᜶ ᜶ ᜶ ɩce; pastoral nomads, such as
those in Tibet, travᴇᴇ ᜶ ᜶ ɩs.

Norbulinga: The summer palacᴇ ᴖᴇ ᜶ ɩ Lama in Lhasa, Tibet.

Oracles: Holy individuals who, it is believed, can predict the future and interpret dreams and visions.

Panchen Lama: The second most holy man in Tibet; the eighth reincarnation lived from 1942 to 1985 and was imprisoned in China for ten years.

People's Liberation Army (PLA): The Communist forces led by Mao Zedong that took China over from the Nationalists in 1949, then became the country's army.

People's Republic of China: The name given to the Communist government that took power in China in 1949.

Potala: The winter palace of the Dalai Lama in Lhasa.

Qing Dynasty: The Manchu Dynasty, which ruled China from 1644 to 1912; sometimes written Ch'ing.

Reincarnation: The belief that the soul is reborn into another body when the previous body dies.

Secular: Nonreligious.

Sharecropper: A tenant farmer who, in exchange for work done, receives a share of value of the crop produced.

Shigatse: Tibet's second-largest city, southwest of Lhasa; it is the capital city of the Panchen Lama.

Sutras: The holy written works of Buddhism.

Taktser: The birthplace of the Dalai Lama in northeastern Tibet; now part of Xinjiang Province, China.

Tenzin Gyatso: The common name of the Dalai Lama; his full name is Jetsun Jamphel Ngawang Lobsang Yeshi Tenzin Gyatso.

Yak: A goatlike animal that lives in the Himalayan Mountains; Tibetans use the yak for clothing, food, milk, and transportation.

Zhou Enlai: A Communist Chinese leader, and the foreign minister of China from 1949 to 1958; sometimes written Chou En-lai.

Bibliography

Avedon, John F. *In Exile from the Land of Snows*. New York: Alfred A. Knopf, 1984. A fine, well-written book that incorporates hundreds of interviews and newspaper articles. Contains an interesting section on traditional Tibetan medicine as well as a chilling account of life in Chinese prisons. Excellent illustrations. Suffers only from a lack of source citations.

_____. *An Interview with the Dalai Lama*. New York: Littlebird, 1980. A brief book, well written and easy to read. Avedon gives the Dalai Lama an opportunity to explain his motives and to clear up misunderstandings about his actions in Tibet from 1950 to 1959.

Goldstein, Melvyn C. *A History of Modern Tibet, 1913-1951: The Demise of the Lamaist State*. Berkeley: University of California Press, 1989. While this is not so much a book about the Dalai Lama as it is a history of Tibet, its description of the political and social system is excellent. The photographs and appendices are also very good.

Goodman, Michael Harris. *The Last Dalai Lama: A Biography*. Boston: Shambala, 1986. Probably the most even-handed book about the Dalai Lama. Goodman uses interviews very well. A little more difficult reading than Avedon's books, but more thorough—Goodman provides sources for facts and quotations, which Avedon does not.

Levenson, Claude B. *The Dalai Lama: A Biography*. Translated by Stephen Cox. London: Unwin Hyman, 1988. Includes valuable insights but suffers from a lack of objectivity. Levenson refers to the Dalai Lama as "Ocean of Wisdom" and "god-king" and devotes large sections to the Buddhist religion. The section entitled "On the Highways of the World" is valuable for its depiction of the Dalai Lama as a globetrotting advocate for a peaceful Tibetan solution.

Piburn, Sidney, ed. *The Dalai Lama, a Policy of Kindness: An Anthology of Writing by and About the Dalai Lama*. Ithaca, New York: Snow Lion, 1990. A collection that includes two Nobel Prize addresses by the Dalai Lama—his lecture and his evening address. Also includes interviews by John Avedon and others as well as talks by the Dalai Lama on religion and environmentalism.

The Utne Reader, March/April, 1989. Special issue entitled "Inside Tibet." A good series of articles with many photographs. John Avedon's "Tibet Today" article is excellent. Also contains an article by two Western doctors who witnessed the September, 1987, crackdown by the Chinese Army.

Ward, Fred. "Visit to Forbidden Tibet." *National Geographic*, February, 1980, pp. 218-259. A very good article written shortly after Tibet was opened to Western visitors in 1979. Ward includes valuable information on both Tibet and the Dalai Lama; good pictures of the land and people.

Wilby, Sorrel. "A Journey Through Tibet." *National Geographic*, December, 1987, pp. 764-785. The story of a woman who walked through Tibet; an interesting account with fine photographs.

Media Resources

Banks, Barbara, and Meg McLagan, producers. *Tibet in Exile*. Video, 30 minutes. 1991. Distributed by The Video Project, Oakland, Calif. Includes footage of the Dalai Lama's escape from Tibet and his activities in exile. Focuses on the lives of ten Tibetan children raised in exile in India. Also contains some rare footage of Chinese attacks on Tibetan monks.

Lung Ta: The Forgotten Tibet. Video, 86 minutes. 1991. Distributed by Zeitgeist Films, New York, N.Y. Produced in France, this is an excellent presentation of the effects of the Chinese occupation of Tibet. Contains some information on the Dalai Lama. Beautifully photographed; narrated by actor Richard Gere.

Moyers: Spirit and Nature. Video, 90 minutes. Public Affairs Television, 1991. Distributed by PBS Video, Alexandria, Va. Commentator Bill Moyers examines the religious and environmental philosophies of the Dalai Lama and other religious leaders, including a Native American elder, at a conference at Middlebury College in Vermont.

Ocean of Wisdom. Video, 30 minutes. Mediart Films and KTEH, 1990. Distributed by PBS Video, Alexandria, Va. Perhaps the best video on the Dalai Lama. This award-winning work examines his life using rare film, videos, and interviews; also shows the suffering of the Tibetan people under Chinese rule.

The Reincarnation of Khensur Rinpoche. Video, 62 minutes. 1991. Distributed by Zeitgeist Films, New York. Traces the search for and discovery of the reincarnation of a Tibetan lama. Includes some discussion of the Dalai Lama, who officially recognized the reincarnation.

A Song for Tibet. Video, 57 minutes. 1991. Distributed by Zeitgeist Films, New York. This Canadian video traces the struggles of the Tibetan community in Montreal to keep its culture alive, especially among the children. Centers on preparations for the 1991 visit of the Dalai Lama to Montreal. Blue ribbon winner at the 1992 American Film Festival.

World Leaders

The Dalai Lama

INDEX

111